Math Game 1

Y. kids

Math Game 1

Copyright © 2005 Sam & Youngin Singapore Pte Ltd.

World rights reserved. No part of this publication may be stored in a retrieval system, transmitted, or reproduced in any way, including but not limited to photocopy, photograph, magnetic, or other record, without the prior agreement and written permission of the publisher.

ISBN: 981-05-2238-X

Printed in the Republic of Korea.

How to contact us

E-mail: feedback@youngjin.com.sg

Address: Youngin Singapore Pte Ltd.
2F, 82 Amoy Street,
Singapore 069901

Telephone: +65-6327-1161
Fax: +65-6327-1151

Manager: Suzie Lee
Acquisition and Developmental Editor: Cris Lee
Copyeditor : Elisabeth Beller
Proofreaders : Elisabeth Beller, Yonie Overton

Story: Tori Jung
Art: Haley Chung
Color: Winsorblue

Book Designer: Litmus
Cover Designer: Namu & Litmus

Math Game 1

Rescue Alice
from the Evil Math King!

sam

Story | Tori Jung
Art | Haley Chung
Color | Winsorblue

Y. kids

The *Math Game* series is not linked to a specific curriculum for children. It is a supplementary tool to help children learn the principles of mathematics naturally through interesting stories. While enjoying the comics, children will discover interesting and real-life aspects of mathematics. There are no supplemental study pages in the text, but the book has been designed in a way that allows children to learn on their own while reading. There is a review section at the end of the book to remind children of what they have learned.

Principles of mathematics are explained thoroughly so that anyone who can read and understand English can understand them. Although this book is intended for third graders or older students, the episodes will be interesting for adults as well.

The storyline is as follows: Children who dislike mathematics speak ill of it. The Evil Math King hears them and is angered. He captures one of the children and then challenges the others to come to Math Land to try to save their friend. The children soon discover the pathway to Math Land, which opens each time they discover a fact of mathematics used in their daily lives. On arriving at Math Land, the children find that they must pass through a number of gates. Each gate is guarded by a master of mathematics who gives out problems the children must solve in order to progress. While passing through each gate, the children get more and more interested in mathematics. Do they finally save their friend? You will find the answer to this question in *Math Game 3*.

Leave this book near children. When they open it, they will discover the world of mathematics!

Math Game 1 contains eight episodes that teach about round numbers, the numbers "0" and "1," Roman numerals, and even and odd numbers.

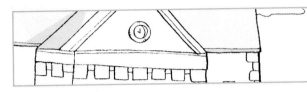

Contents

Well, you two look cozy...

Oh!
No, please!!

Hmph! If I were you, I'd pay attention in math class rather than passing notes to one another.

Hehe...
Sorry...
We won't do it again.

Gasp!
What the...?!!

It doesn't matter whether you like me or not. That is entirely up to you, but I will not tolerate students who do not pay attention in my class. Jimmy and Alice, you two will remain after school and work on math problems.

Yes, Ms. Rodriguez...

We'll never finish this!

Tell me about it. This is all because of math!

I hate math. I get all cranky and angry when it comes time for math and look what happened!

You too? I get the same way.

If there is such a place as Math Land, then I bet the king of that place is one evil and nasty dude! Why'd he have to go and make up this kind of subject anyway?!

Yeah! I'd like to give that old Math King a piece of my mind!

Hey! You guys still not done yet?! Will you hurry up already?!

Yeah, I'm hungry! We're outta here! See ya later!

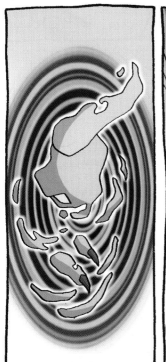

Some friends you are!

Who dares curse me?!

Wh-who are you?

I am the Evil Math King.

Ahhh! There really is such a thing as a Math King...?!

I've been listening to your conversation and I've heard just about enough! Who dared curse me?!

Was it you?

Oh no! I don't even know any bad words.

Then, was it you?

Of course not! I never even knew that there was such a thing as an evil Math King.

Wh-what am I going to do...?

Now I remember.
I heard a girl's voice.
It was you!!

Ack!! Please spare me! Spare me!! I won't say bad things about you anymore!!

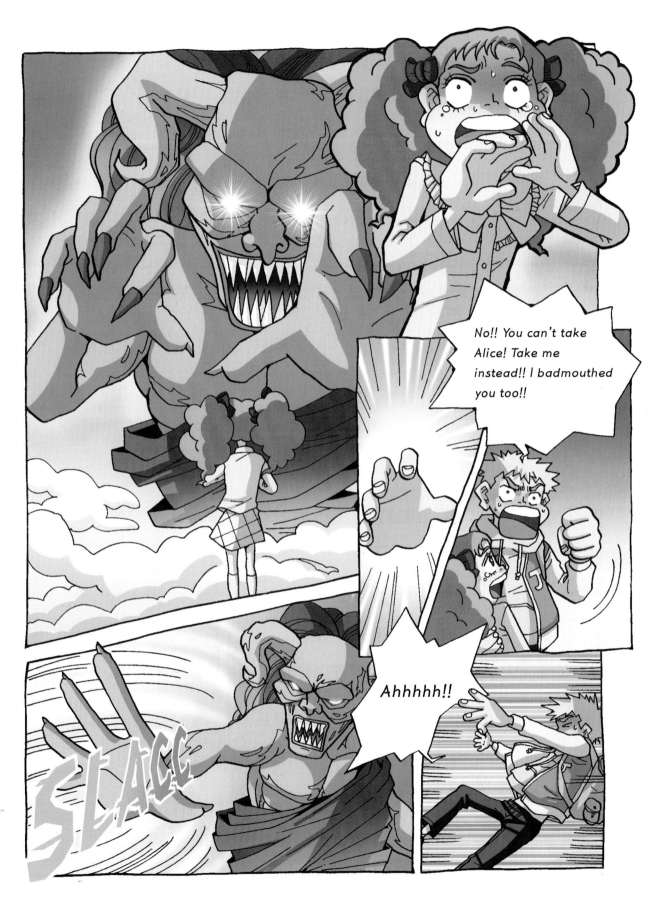

I only take one prisoner.
The one who has cursed me the most...!

Alice! Alice!!

Ahhh! I'm so scared! You guys, help me!!

Ugh...! Alice! Alice!!

Alice! Alice!!

The Math King let her return!

Alice! Alice! Wake up!!

EPISODE 2
Save Alice!

Over here, Jimmy!

Looks like you got here before me.

Let's go to Math Land!!

Do you even know where Math Land is?

No...

Then how are we supposed to get there?!

Well, then do you have any other ideas? We'll just have to go!! We have to go save Alice!!

Ugh! This is so frustrating! We still have to find out where Math Land is.

Yeah, Colby's got a point. Let's take a look at the world map.

Papua, New Guinea. Fiji. Solomon's Island...

It's not here. It's not here. We've even looked through all the small islands, and there's no such place as Math Land.

We've been searching for two hours. Maybe it's not in the school after all.

I can't look anymore.

I can't find it!! Where's the stupid path to Math Land anyway?!

GROWL

How about we stop for a bite to eat?

How can you think about food at a time like this? We have to save Alice!

Okay. We'll stop for a snack and then start looking again.

Good idea! Good idea! We need our strength, don't we?

BURGER

IN

Let me see! What do I want?

I want a cheeseburger.

I want a shrimp burger.

Okay. Two cheeseburgers and one shrimp burger—that's $3.00. A chicken nugget meal is $5.00, and an order of fries is $1.00, bringing the total to $9.00! Everyone chip in $3.00 each.

Look over there. We've finally found the passageway to Math Land!!

Wake up, will ya? This ain't your bedroom, you know.

Yaawn! That was a great nap. But where are we?

What do you mean "where are we"? This is Math Land!

Are you brave or just stupid?

Hey, Jimmy! How'd you know that that hole that opened up at Burger Land would bring us to Math Land?

Yeah, how'd you know that?

Umm... Well...???

Well, the Evil Math King did say that we would find the passage to Math Land in a place that was closely related to math!

What does Burger Land have to do with Math Land?

Yeah, I'd figure Burger Land would be closer to Food Land or something like that.

Yeah, or Hungry Land... Giggle!

Why are you looking at me?!

Hehe! No reason! No reason at all!

Thanks to Sam, we were able to find Math Land!!!

Okay, now that we're here in Math Land, let's go look for Alice.

Okay! Let's go!

Team Alice, here we go!!

Look! I see an oasis!!

Where?

Where?

Hehe! If the legends are right...
then that's just a mirage. Kekeke!!

Hehehe!!

Omph!

We found it!

Is...is that Math Land?

I-I'm scared!

GATE 1

EPISODE 3
Round Numbers

I'm glad you've come. I welcome you to the first gate to Math Land.

Excuse me? Do you mean to tell me that this isn't Math Land?

Hehehe! So you think it's that easy to get to Math Land, huh? You're only at the first gate.

Oh my gosh!

Shoot! I never expected it to be so hard to get to Math Land!

How many gates are there in all?

Hehehe! I don't know. I'm just the first gatekeeper...

Abracadabra- twirly-wirly- cha cha cha!

6,148,512,782

What's that?

And what are those numbers?

How much is that...? 1, 2, 3... carry the one...

Okay, now I shall give you the real problem.

What?! That wasn't the real question?

Did you expect the questions to be that easy?!

Hmph! We got all excited for nothing?

Tell me about it.

This number is the earth's population. That's how many people live on Earth today!

6,148,512,782

6,148,512,783

You're the gatekeeper??!

Uh-huh. Don't I look much better without the mask on?

Why were you wearing that gross mask in the first place?

Yeah! Why were you?

I just wanted to add an element of fear. You know, like in the movies. This is called...drama!

How did you know about round numbers?

What?! Is that what they're called?!

What are Round Numbers?

A round number is not an accurate value but an approximate value. We also call them "round figures," or "approximate numbers." Round numbers are used when you don't know the exact number of something or when you do know the exact number, but you don't need to use the complete exact number. For example, let's suppose that the exact population of a village is 17,142. Instead of saying "the population is 17,412," we can simply say that there are approximately 17,000 people living in the village.

EPISODE-4
The Discovery of Zero

Children, I'm afraid I have some bad news. Alice is very sick, and she won't be able to come to school.

Alice is sick?

She is? Maybe we should go visit her after school.

No, you can't visit her. She isn't awake yet!

What?! It's that bad?!

No. The doctor says that Alice is physically fine. Don't worry. She'll come out of her coma soon.

Now that school's over, let's go to Math Land.

Yes! Today we must try to pass the second gate!

Let's go!!

Let's look for a place that's closely related to math.

Hehe! I bet I find it again this time.

Not if I can help it! I'll find it this time!!

THUD!
THUD!

Whew!
That was close.

Whew! We would have been flattened by that thing!

Where are we?

I'm just guessing, but I think we're in ancient Rome.

I think you're right. I've seen chariots like that in the movies.

What?! Ancient Rome?!

Are you sure this is the question for the second gate?

Yes!

That's an elevator...

Then the answer is...!!

The only possible answer is zero. But then, it's too easy. Do you think it's a trap?

That's what I was thinking.

What?! A...a trap !!

We can't follow them! It's too dangerous?!

Yeah, Sam's right. Didn't you see their big swords?

Then what are we supposed to do? Without him, we can't go back home or continue on to Math Land!!

......

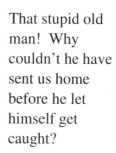

That stupid old man! Why couldn't he have sent us home before he let himself get caught?

Gasp!
What's that?!

Ahhhhh!!

EPISODE 5
Roman Numerals

Me? Okay...um...1993.

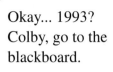

Okay... 1993?
Colby, go to the
blackboard.

Can you write
down that number
in Roman
numerals?

Huh?!

Use this as your guide.

Is it difficult? Okay then, watch me.
This is how you write the year "1993."

Woooooaaaa!!
That's too hard!

Okay, now let me explain.

First, "M" stands for "one thousand."
Next, we have "9" in the hundreds
place. In Roman numerals, when a
digit is written on the left side of
another digit, we subtract it. So, since
900 is 1000 - 100, we write "CM."

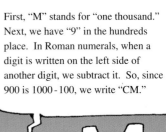

Looking back at this chart I made, we can see that "C" is "100" and "X" is "10." Since "100 - 10 = 90," we write "XC" here.

That brings us to "1990"...

And then we add "III" to express "1993" in Roman numerals as MCMXCIII!

Wow~!

Now I know how important the number "0" is.

Yeah! The Romans were stupid.

Yeah. Can you imagine how mad they'd be if they knew that in the future, their precious Roman numerals were only used on cuckoo clocks?!

That reminds me! We have to go to Math Land again!

Yes! It's off to Gate 3!!

No, I mean to Gate 2!

We already passed Gate 2!!

No. We have to go save that old man!

What?!

We have to show those Romans that the truth always wins!

Oh! Hi, Tony. Hi, Hogan!

What are you doing here?

Why don't I show you guys a hard time?!

I'd prefer it if you didn't act like that in front of me again.

Quick, you guys! Run!

Ahh! Those brats!!!

Gasp, gasp, gasp!

What's with those guys! Gasp! Gasp!!

Yeah! What'd we ever do to them? Gasp, gasp!

Who cares if they're the smartest and strongest in the class?!

Isn't that strange?!

What?

Zero comes before one, and people consider it to be an important number, but why is the number "1" always used to refer to "the best"?

Ugh...
Where are we?!

I don't know. Do you think we made it back to the Roman Empire?

Gasp! I—it's a c-cobra!!

I've seen things like this before...

That means... we're in India!

But where's Sam?

How come he's always getting lost!

Sam! Sam!

Yawwwn!

Sam!!

What a great nap!!

Sam, look down and see what you're lying on?

What do you mean, what I'm lying on? I'm probably just lying down on the ground.

Ahhhh!!

Ouch!! It stings!!

We should've just let him sleep...

Again I ask, is he thick skinned or just thickheaded?

SACK OF RICE
105 RUPEES

250 RUPEES

Huh?
The people
in India use
the number "0."

Yeah. Remember
when the second
gatekeeper asked
us if we were from
India or Arabia?

I guess that means
that the Indians
began using zero
before the Romans
did.

The Indians must
be very good
at math.

Who are they? They are dressed in strange costumes.

They saw us! Run!!

Gasp!! It's a dead end!!

Hello and welcome to the third gate of Math Land.

Finally! We're at the third gate.

It wasn't so painful this time.

Is there any way we can return to the second gate?

Why's that?

We want to help the second gatekeeper.

Don't be absurd! If you go save him, you'll be changing the course of history as we know it! The past is past! You must not change even the smallest event, no matter how insignificant!!

But I feel sorry for him.

There's nothing you can do about it. If the Romans refuse to accept the number "0," their development in mathematics will inevitably be slower...

......

There's no way the Romans will be able to keep up with the Indians when it comes to math. Not after all I went through to discover the number "0"...!

Yes. I am the mathematician who discovered zero.

Are you sure about that?

What's that look for?

Are you sure you're not confused? Maybe your specialty is yoga and not math?

Hrrrmph!

Could we please just focus on the question?

I was so touched by Jimmy's caring heart that I was going to let you pass easily, but forget it now!

Yapdara wapdara sharp points!

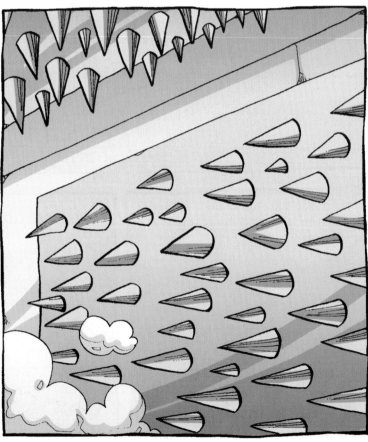

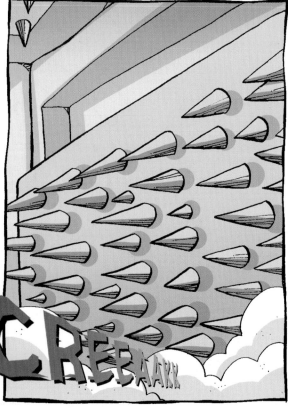

Here is my question. I'm sure you can guess what will happen to you if you give me the wrong answer. Hehehe!

......

Why is the number "1" used to represent the best? First place! No. 1! #1!...

That's what I asked before...!

So now we move from zero to one...?

*People believed that at the turn of the millenium, computers wouldn't be able to recognize the year "2000" and that this would create problems around the world. Fortunately, it did not turn out to be a problem.

So then doesn't the twenty-first century begin with the year 2000?!

Yeah. This isn't a test of math. It's a test of memory. Let's just answer the question.

No! Something doesn't feel right about this. It feels like a trap.

What?! Another trap?!

Yeah. Think back to the other gates. The obvious answer has never been the right answer.

But, Jimmy, things are different now. If the twenty-first century starts with the year 2001, then that means we've all had it wrong all this time!!

Yeah! Yeah!!

The answer is the year 2000!

What's your reason for choosing the year 2000?

Everyone in the world believes that the year 2000 is the start of the new millennium... I've seen it on TV and in newspapers.

Ho ho ho! And how is your answer related to math?

Huh?!

You're not going to tell me that everyone in the entire world is wrong, are you?

Ho ho! Math is about the truth. Math does not care what the public thinks. A long time ago, people believed that the sun rotated around the earth. Did you know that?

However, only the mathematician Galileo Galilei supported the theory that the earth circled the sun.

He was even in trouble with the church for his beliefs.

It was discovered later that Galileo was indeed right. No matter how much the people failed to believe him, the truth was the truth, although supporting the truth can get quite lonely sometimes. And math is also about the truth.

Then...?!

Yes, the twenty-first century does begin with the year 2001.

H-how is that possible?!

I don't know. No one's ever told me that before!!

The world of math is not controlled by popular belief but by the truth!

You are wrong! No wrong answers are permitted in Math Land! Hahahaha!!

CREEAAK

Gasp! What're we gonna do?!

Ahhhh! We're dead now!

This is all my fault...!

The number "1" is the oldest of all the numbers! It is the only number that can be divided into all other numbers, but no other number can be divided into it!

The number "1" is also used to refer to kings and leaders.

The number "1" has given birth to all the other numbers and is where all numbers start.

Run to where
the old man is!

Huh?
Oh, yeah, OK!

How'd you get out of there?!

EPISODE 7
The Extra Question

Were you really going to kill us?

Yeah! We're the main characters of this book. If we die, the book ends here!

Yeah! I don't think that old man has seen many movies!

I'm just following orders...

You should know to think for yourself, too!

Yeah! Where's your backbone!

Yes, sir, oh great Evil Math King!!
Yes! Yes! Yes!

Wait!
Let me
talk to him!!

Evil Math King, return Alice to us at once!!

Oh no!!

I've just spoken with the Evil Math King. There is one way you guys can get out of here.

What is it?

Tell us quickly.

You shall receive your punishment.

What? Punishment!!

Open
soybean!

Be quiet!
If you want to get out of here, you will count them!!

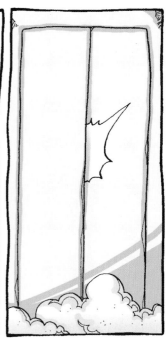

Shoot! By the time we finish counting all these, we'll need canes to walk out of here!

Yeah. And if we make a mistake, we'll have to start over. This is all a trick to have us starve to death in here!

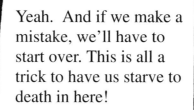

What can I do?
What can I do...?!

RUMBLING!

I'm going to die of hunger!

Mommy!

Alice, I'm sorry! I'm sorry I couldn't save you...

That's right. I have some candy with me.

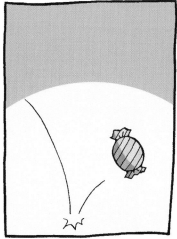

Uh oh... There's only one piece of candy left.

It isn't big enough to split into threes. Oh well, I need my strength.

Alright!
Alright!!
I'll share!!

That's it!
All we need is
this!!

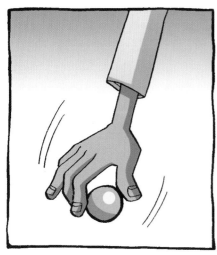

You're supposed to share during hard times, you know!!

I was gonna share...

Oh really? Of course you were. I'll keep this safe here and divide it up when we really need it.

Shoot!

Hey! Come over here!

What's the matter? Did you come up with an idea?!

What's he so happy about...?

You guys, count these.

What for?!

This is no time for games, Jimmy.

Just count them. Here, I'll divide them up into three piles so that we can all count them together.

I have 274! What about you, Colby?

I've got 256.

And you, Sam?

302.

Now, you're sure about that, right? Good. Adding up our totals, we get 832.

Whew! Done. That's 72 bagfuls of beans with 132 left over!

Hey, you guys! I've finally counted all the beans.

Jimmy, are you serious?

Jimmy, if you're wrong, we're dead for sure.

No, I'm sure. Let's get out of here.

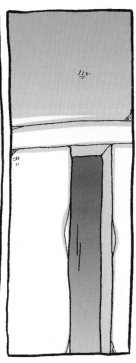

I have no tolerance for liars.

Of course you don't!

If you're lying to me and guessed instead of counting the beans, I'll add another baleful of beans to the pile!!

With this!!

Of course. We've counted them, I tell you.

What?! How'd you count them so fast?

Jimmy...

A total of 832 beans were placed in the empty bag. There were 72 bags of beans in total. So that's 832 × 72 = 59,904 beans. Add to that the 132 beans left over, and there is a total of 60,036 beans in all.

$$832 \times 72 = 59,904$$

$$132 + 59,904 = 60,036$$

That was great, Jimmy!

I knew you could do it!!

Hoo hoo hoo...!

It was a great idea to use multiplication to find the answer. In math, the process of getting to the answer is as important as the answer itself. However, Jimmy has made a fatal mistake.

What do you mean a fatal mistake...?

How do you know that there are 832 beans in the empty bag?

There'll be times when you'll have more or less than that number!!

I have a question.

What is it?

I heard that the number "0" was discovered in India. That must mean that you are very good in math, so how come India wasn't the first country to send a rocket to the moon?

That's because...

AHHHHH...

EPISODE 8
Odd and Even

Does that mean that people in lower castes didn't receive an education?

I guess you could say that.

Not even in math?

Math? Math was the least of their worries in the past.

Aha! Now I get it.

What do you get, Jimmy?

It's nothing.

No, I'm curious. If you've realized something, please share it with the class so that we can all learn.

You know that the number "0" was discovered in India, right??

Mmhm... Of course.

I used to wonder how come India, a country that is so good in math, wasn't the first country to send a rocket to the moon.

And?

Now I know why. It's because of the caste system.

In India, math was not used by all the people but only by privileged people of higher castes. That's why math wasn't able to develop as much as it could have.

That makes sense...

Yeah! That's it!

We never were able to hear that old man's answer, but now I know.

But India is changing and is now one of the leaders in information technology. All that aside, Jimmy, you are showing an incredible interest in math lately. That's great.

Hey!
let's play
odds and evens!

Odd!

*Puhahaha!
No, uh–uh!
It's even!!*

Hey, Colby!
Let's play
odds and evens.

I'm busy.
I have to go.

Chicken!
Too
afraid to
face
me...?

*What?!
Alright!
Bring
it on!!*

Even!

Alright!
Now open
your hand.

What are you doing?! Get your hands off me!!

What's the matter? All you have to do is open your hand...

Alright! Alright already!

Yahoo!! It's even!! Even!

Since I won all Hogan's money today, I'll treat you guys to something! What do you want?

You didn't win. It was all thanks to Jimmy.

Whatever...

That Hogan is so bad. He cheats all the kids out of their money!

You did good. He deserved it!

Jimmy! Sam! Get over here, quick!

What's the matter, Colby?

Tony and Hogan are waiting for us!

Let me at them! I'll teach them a thing or two!!

Not today. We'll walk around.

What's the matter? What are you afraid of? I'm not afraid of them.

People walk around a piece of poop on the ground because it's filthy, not because they're scared!

Yeah, Sam. But they'll be furious when they learn that we took another route home today.

Let's use the gap in the wall behind the school.

You little weasels!

Wasn't I right, Hogan?
I knew they'd try
to escape.
You think I wouldn't
know you'd try to
escape through here?

Give me back my money!!

What are you talking about?!
It's not your money!

You cheated me! So give me back my money!

You're the one who's cheating the other kids!!

Wh—what?!! I'm no cheater!

This leads to a dead end.

Yeah.

What are we going to do?

There's only
one thing to do.

What?

What is it?

Math Land!!

*Yeah!
That's it!*

Again?

This time, we'll think of something to open up the passage into Math Land. Hurry! Think!

I can't think of math just like that!

Math! Math!!

What did we do today that was closest to math?

I'm not sure. We didn't even have math today...

All you did was play odds and evens with Hogan during break time.

Yeah. Odd numbers start out 1, 3, 5, 7, 9...

And even numbers start out 2, 4, 6, 8...

Hmm...have you ever wondered if, the higher up we count, odd numbers will be bigger than even numbers? Or maybe the even numbers will be bigger than the odd numbers...

I don't know. I think odd numbers might be bigger...

No, since even numbers start with 2, wouldn't even numbers be bigger...?

We did it!

Yup! Math can always be found around us!

Puhahaha! Catch us if you can, boys!!

Gasp, gasp, gasp! Where'd they go?!

They got away again?!!

To be continued in Math Game 2!

◎ Round Numbers

A round number is not an exact number. It is an "approximation," as when you say someone is "about five feet tall" when yon know that they are actually a little taller or a little shorter.

Round numbers can be used when you don't know the exact number or when you know the exact number, but you don't need to use it.

Example: Suppose that there are exactly 17,140 people living in a town. If someone asks you how many people live in that town, you probably wouldn't say the exact number. You would probably round the number and say that there are about 17,000 people living in that town.

We can round numbers up or round them down. In most cases, we round to the nearest whole number.

1. Rounding a Number Up

First look at the digit you want to round (the "rounding digit") and then look to the right of it. If the digit to the right is greater than or equal to 1, add the number "1" to the rounding digit and then change all digits to the right to zeros.

Example: Let's round 17,140 **up** to the next hundred. The rounding digit is 1 and since the digit to the right—4—is greater than 1, we add 1 to the rounding digit and our rounded answer is 17,200.

2. Rounding a Number Down

Look again at your rounding digit. The rounding digit and all digits to the left of the rounding digit can be left alone. Change all digits to the right to zeros.

Example: Let's round 17,140 **down** to the nearest hundred. The rounding digit is, again, 1. We leave that alone, and we change all digits to the right to zeros, which gives us 17,100.

3. Rounding to the Nearest Whole Number

If you are asked to round to the nearest whole number, you might have to round up or round down. How do you decide which one to do?

You will want to round **up** if the digit to the right of the rounding digit is greater than or equal to 5. If this is the case, you add 1 to the rounding digit and replace all the digits to the right of it with zeros.

You will want to round **down** if the digit to the right of the rounding digit is less than 5. If that is the case, you keep the rounding digit as it is and you replace all digits to the right of it with zeros.

Example: Let's round 17,140 to the nearest hundred. The rounding digit is 1. Since the digit to the right—4—is less than 5, we round **down**, and the rounded answer is 17,100. But if our original number had been 17,160, the digit to the right of the rounding number would have been greater than 5, and we would have rounded **up**, making our rounded answer 17,200.

There probably aren't many of you who've thought a lot about zero, but the number "0" can be quite interesting.

Whether we are adding, subtracting, multiplying, dividing, or solving math problems, we can see that the number "0" is quite special.

Example: No matter how many zeros we add up, the result (or "sum") will always be zero. No matter how complex or large a number may be, if we multiply it by zero, the result (or "product") will be zero. We also see that no number can be divided into zero.

So what makes zero so special?

Usually, we use the number "0" to refer to nothingness (as in "zip" or "zilch"). Does that mean that zero only stands for nothingness?

Before we answer that question, let's look at the origin of zero.

Zero was used in India many hundreds of years ago. The earliest mention of zero in Indian literature dates back to 876 AD. A dot (●) may have been used to represent zero before this time. Later, the number "0" was added to the system of Arabic numbers (1, 2, 3, ...), and its use spread slowly to other regions of the world. Mayan mathemeticians (in what would become southern Mexico and parts of Central America) also used a symbol for zero in 665 AD or even earlier, but their use of zero did not spread to other cultures.

Let's take another look at the different meanings of zero. In elementary school, we use zero in math problems: If you have three apples and your brother eats three apples, how many apples do you have left? The answer is 3 - 3 = 0. So from examples like this, we learn to think of zero as nothingness.

But zero is so much more. Imagine a thermometer. On a thermometer, 0° centigrade does not refer to a state of "no" temperature; it is simply the very center of the thermometer. In other words, 15° centigrade is fifteen degrees higher than 0° centigrade, and -15° centigrade is fifteen degrees lower than 0° centigrade.

What about telephone numbers? A lot of telephone numbers have the number "0" in them, but here the number "0" does not refer to nothingness or to the center of something. Here, zero is simply another number like one, two, or three. And in money, zero is used as a place marker that helps you know the value of the money. (We all know that adding a few zeros to $10 to make it $10,000 makes a big difference!)

There have been quite a few interesting and amusing stories about zero in history. For example, the numbers we use today (1, 2, 3, ...) are called Arabic numerals, but if we look at some clocks, we can see that they use Roman numerals (I, II, III, ...) rather than Arabic numerals. What are Roman numerals?

Roman numerals were invented by the ancient Romans. There are seven Roman numerals (but there is no Roman numeral for zero). The numerals are I (which equals 1), V (5), X (10), L (50), C (100), D (500), and M (1,000). These seven Roman numerals can be combined in different ways to represent any number. That's because each Roman numeral represents a definite value, and that value doesn't change no matter where the symbol is placed in a number. In other words, the Arabic numeral "1," has one value when it appears in the number "10" but another value in the number "100." However, the Roman numeral "C" will always be "100" no matter where it is placed.

◎ Roman Numerals

Here are the Roman numerals from one to twenty:

1	2	3	4	5	6	7	8	9	10	11	12	13	14	15	16	17	18	19	20
I	II	III	IV	V	VI	VII	VIII	IX	X	XI	XII	XIII	XIV	XV	XVI	XVII	XVIII	XIX	XX

Here are the rest of the Roman numerals:

50	100	500	1,000
L	C	D	M

Roman numerals are generally read from left to right. The Roman numeral "I," (which is "1"), originated from a single finger. "V" (which is "5") represents the space between the thumb and the index finger when all five fingers of one hand are spread out.

One theory for "X" (which is "10") is that just as five is half of ten, so the Roman numeral for five, "V," is the top half of the Roman numeral "X."

Roman numerals are fairly easy to translate into Arabic numerals. Remember that you simply read them from left to right and always start with the largest unit.

Example:

CCLXVII = 100 + 100 + 50 + 10 + 5 + 1 + 1 = 267

MMCCLXXXI = 1,000 + 1,000 + 100 + 100 + 50 + 10 + 10 + 10 + 1 = 2281

Larger numbers (like 31,425) are a different story. Since the largest unit in Roman numerals is "M" (1,000), in order to write 31,425 using Roman numerals, we would have to write "M" thirty-one times!

Here's another interesting fact. Some Roman numerals are expressed as subtractions. For example, instead of expressing the number "4" as "IIII," it is expressed as "5 - 1" or "IV," where the smaller Roman numeral on the left is subtracted from the larger Roman numeral on the right. Using this same method, "9" would be written "IX."

The complexity of Roman numerals may be why they have been replaced by the Arabic numbers we use today, but they are still an important part of history.

◎ The Mysterious Number One

The number "1" is the only number, except for zero, that can divide any number but cannot be divided by any other number.

Since the number "1" was the first of all the numbers, it was used to refer to kings and leaders. The number "1" was also thought of as the beginning of all things.

When you think about size or numbers of things, the number "1" can mean that something is very small (although if you gather enough together, you may have something very big as in the saying, "Every trip begins with the first step"). The number "1" is the only number that can be defined in these two opposing ways—as a very small unit and as a thing of great importance.

The number "1" can also suggest isolation or aloneness, sameness, or being at the very top of something!

◎ Natural Numbers

One way to think of natural numbers is that they refer to anything you can count in the world around us—flowers, animals, and people, for example—so we can define natural numbers as "numbers used to count or order things."

Natural numbers are positive (that is, greater than zero) whole numbers such as 1, 2, 3, 4, and so on. Natural numbers can be added and multiplied to make other natural numbers, but subtraction and division of natural numbers may not result in other natural numbers.

Example: The result of 3 -5 is -2, which is not a natural number because it is a negative number (less than zero).

◎ Even and Odd Numbers

Even numbers are whole numbers that can be divided by the number "2," such as-6, -4, -2, 0, 2, 4, 6, and so on. "Odd numbers" are whole numbers that are not evenly divisible by the number "2," such as -5, -3, -1, 1, 3, 5, 7, and so on.

When you add or subtract two odd numbers, the result is always an even number. When you multiply or divide two odd numbers, if the result is a whole number, it is always an odd number.